Six Days in St. Petersburg

A CHRONICLE OF RETURN

Six Days in St. Petersburg

A CHRONICLE OF RETURN

poems by

ALLA RENÉE BOZARTH

PURPLE IRIS PRESS
Los Angeles, California

Front cover design © 1993 by Cynthia A. Clark

ISBN 1-883230-03-9

All photographs are reprinted courtesy of the author, except the photographs on page 31 and the back cover, courtesy of Julia Barkley.

Portions of *The Great Path of Awakening*, by Jamgon Kongtrul, "The Root Text of the Seven Points of Training the Mind", translated by the Nalada Translation Committee, © 1987 by Ken McLeod, are reprinted by arrangement with Shambhala Publications, Inc., 300 Massachusetts Ave., Boston, MA 02115.

Inquiries, orders, and catalog requests should be addressed to:

PURPLE IRIS PRESS
1015 Gayley Avenue, Suite 237
Los Angeles, California 90024-3424
U.S.A.
310/478-5599

For Alvina Heckel DeGolikov Bozarth

-- "Mama" --

with a grateful heart

Alvina Heckel DeGolikov Bozarth, in Russia as a young woman.

TABLE OF CONTENTS

Prolegomena

Six Days in St. Petersburg

Afterword

Preface

In January 1992, a trip to Russia was the furthest thing from my mind. On March 27, I was off to St. Petersburg with my friend Julia Barkley, a visual artist who has collaborated with me on two books of poems and paintings, and a gift to the people of Hiroshima of poetry and paintings for the permanent collection in the Peace Memorial Garden -- the first such works by foreign women artists.

Julia had found an excellent tour package for us, making a dream of our seventeen-year friendship come true. I had never told her that I was secretly reluctant, if not afraid, to go to Russia with her. I kept in mind the stories my mother had told me of our family's suffering after the Revolution, and the deaths and gulag experiences under Stalin. I still had relatives in internal exile in Siberia as late as the 1970s! My visit with my mother to East Berlin in 1965 had left memory scars. Images of Soviet soldiers still haunted my dreams.

But in the early spring of 1992, everything was changed. Russia was in chaos, to be sure, and the Russian people were worried, to say the least. But Russia was Russia again!

My mother was born in Odessa on the Black Sea in 1909. Her mother and younger brother fled as refugees to Canada soon after the Revolution. Mama followed them in 1929. Before she left Russia, she studied and worked for a time in Moscow, learning costume design and acting in a Soviet film in the mid-twenties. In Canada, she learned English and performed with the Prime Minister's Acting Company. Later, she sought fame on Broadway, but went the way of many young actors of her day, starving in Morningside Heights instead. Her Prince found and married her -- Dmitri DeGolikov, of the royal house of Rhyzhevsky-Smolensky. His heart was weak, so he sold his Russian restaurant in New York and Mama took him to California. She made several screen tests there. I have pictures of her, looking radiant and romantic, a Russian Garbo. But again her art was thwarted. She designed and made clothes for the movie stars, and that was as close as she got to the silver screen.

After Dmitri died, Mama fell in love with my father's voice over the radio. She took drama classes from him, and within weeks they were married. The following spring, I was born. By then, they had left Los Angeles and moved to Portland for my father's new job.

Papa had his own program late at night on radio station KWJJ, at that time a classical station. He performed poetry and played classical and romantic music to accompany his theme, "Of Words and Verse." He became known for his skills as an interviewer of celebrities passing through Portland. When I was little, I knew Norman Thomas and Eleanor Roosevelt. Through his contacts he met an Episcopal priest with whom he became fast friends, and this led to the end of his radio career. He was ordained an Episcopal priest the year that I was to turn four, and my mother was to sponsor the first of hundreds of refugee families who came to the United Stated through her efforts. This family was that of her own first cousin, her older brother's best friend growing up in the rich farmland of the Ukraine.

My mother's work through Church World Service evolved into an immense network of rescue and resettlement of displaced persons from countries in chaos, beginning with her own people coming out of what was once Russia. In my childhood, I went with her to greet families arriving in the early morning at Portland's Union Station. These families were Russian, German, Cuban, Hungarian, Indonesian. Always, she worked to get her remaining relatives in the Soviet Union out to a free place. She wrote many letters to Krushchev, appealing on behalf of her cousin Lucy in Novosibersk. Only after Mama's death did her efforts bear fruit. I know that she lived always in grief for the land of her childhood.

Late one night shortly before I was to meet Julia in New York to begin our great adventure, I thought suddenly that I should take something of my mother's and leave it in Russia as a sign of her return through me. Never had she dreamed that Russia would be Russia again. Now it had happened. I chose to take a tiny photograph of her at the age of fourteen, still living on her family's estate near Odessa. Then I noticed the date: March 23, exactly twenty years from the day of her death in exile. I left for Russia on March 27, the anniversary of Mama's funeral at the little Russian Orthodox Church of St. Nicholas in Portland, where I was baptized in 1947.

I knew of only one place vital to my journey in St. Petersburg. It was the Church of St. Nicholas, and the reason was that I had seen on public television a film about the life of the great poet Anna Akhmatova, whose funeral was illegally filmed there. Akhmatova was born in Odessa twenty years before my mother, but she spent her adult life in St. Petersburg. On the morning following our arrival, I asked our guide if it would be possible to visit this church. She looked at me strangely, then replied, "It is the first place I am taking you."

We came into the snowy courtyard of the church at noon. Through the iron gate we entered the church. Candle flames broke through the darkness. Icons of great age glowed golden at every pillar. A liturgy was taking place. The old ones prayed. It was a Service for the Dead. There, enrapt and humbled, I gave thanks for living at this moment in history, gave thanks for my mother's life, for my ancestors who had lived and died in this immense country; imagined the suffering which had preceded me, the suffering around me, the suffering yet to come, and was overwhelmed. I imagined Anna Akhmatova praying here, making her poems here, being kissed Goodbye here. I felt myself a small part of a great tradition, and was to the core of my bones grateful.

Days later, I found a spot to bury my mother's picture -- near the tombstone of Rimsky-Korsakov. All the while, the bells of his triumphant Easter Liturgy music rang in the marrow of my soul. I had felt "sent," and now my mission was accomplished. These poems ran out of me like little streams of tenderness, gratitude, and care, swelling into rivers of joy and a great reservoir of compassion. They are the map of my pilgrimage to the land of my ancestors.

Prolegomena

REFUGEE WOMEN

Daughters of immigrant women --
this is how it begins,
the evocation of a common
history, a color, a certain
reticence about the self,
a certain cultural separateness.

I realize you do not know
so many aspects of me, your friend
of decades, beginning with:
She was a refugee.
A refugee, not an immigrant,
my mother.

My grandmother fled:
the burning, the desecration
of home, the murdering
of children: the boy's throat
slit where he worked in the flour mill,
the typhoid that killed his mother,
her sister's madness in the concentration
camp, starvation.
These are my relatives,
one generation away.

Stalin's purge.
The millions hated simply
for being, without regard
to character, but hated
for their ancestors
(your people and mine),
hated for their land, hated
for their industry and art,
hated for thinking.
Hated for elegance, for beauty.

Hated for love.
My people -- uncles, aunts,
cousins, grandfathers, mystic
ghosts left in their bodies,
or crazed corpses.

Grandmother survived the famine
and failed crops by making vodka
for the cossacks, then hid
the children from bayonets
by night and fled, under straw,
under rivers of horror, across
the sea, into my future.

When I was eighteen, Mama took me
to Europe on her mother's inheritance.
When we were crossing the border into
(then) East Germany at midnight, red neon
hammer and sickle glaring through rain
at the train stations, she told me
(for the first time!) we had cousins
still in Siberia, still prisoners,
those not murdered, those not made mad,
still confined for a lifetime
to internal exile.
I will never know their stories.

You are right.
We are reticent.
We are psychically unsafe.
We do not always remember to notice
whether we are in a danger zone
or among friends, and sometimes
confuse the heart of a friend with a foe.

My passport was confiscated
on the other side of the Wall in Berlin.

The Russian soldiers scowled at me
and whispered. I was scared silent.
My mind was already frozen in salt mines
and slavery. Only after being detained
and searched did I realize
they had confiscated my breath as well.

Years later, making my stand as a woman,
setting my small mark on history,
the hate mail came, the obscene phone calls,
the stink bombs and death threats,
not because of my character, but because
of what I am and my daring to transcend
the condemnation of what I am.

Only now do I understand
why I was not surprised.
We daughters of refugee women
half expect such things.
We make ourselves safe, find refuge,
migrate like birds to warmer places,
and embrace our lives and our holiness
any way we can.

Six Days in
St. Petersburg

RETURN

My friend stands
on a street corner
in Tel Aviv
at ten o'clock
in the morning to talk
to me before I take
the plane to St. Petersburg.
Yes! It's Petersburg again,
my friend, and I go for your mother and mine
to the land of their origins,
returning for them,
returning for all who cannot
return.

In the background
over the telephone
across ten thousand miles
I hear your blessing,
your warm breath mingle
with the sounds of traffic,
a world too full
of lonely people
crying out for company,
trying to arrive
somewhere.

AT KENNEDY AIRPORT

A city unto itself, a grey island,
a concrete space station.
How depressing.
Exactly as I left it
the summer of '62, thirty years ago.
Only dirtier.
Broken cinder blocks of stairs,
no place to sit but the filthy floor.
Like the Underground, the El,
or a bus station.
These people pay big bucks
to fly around.
Now, like me, even first class
passengers sit on the floor or walk
from terminal to terminal for the nine hours
wait between flights, or give up
their shirts for a scalding cup of stale coffee.
The natives are unkind to travelers,
but more so to each other.
This saddens me.
They have to live together
and they don't know how.
Hostility for hospitality.
Hostile for hostel.
Everything's inside out, inverted.

I drink water from a styrofoam cup
for three hours in the cafeteria
of American Airlines, stake out
my safety zone.

A black security guard in gold earrings
yells and swears at a Hispanic visitor.
(That was when I threw away my half-eaten muffin.)

7

I smiled in both directions and shrugged.
Opening my book, *The Great Path of Awakening*
(chosen for its travel-friendly thinness),
the pages open randomly near the end,
my preferred starting point. I read:
"Rest in the nature of *alaya*, the essence,"
I do so now. It is my name, after all.
Deciding then to send out love
to all living beings in this place
and make my small peace-offering, I read on:
"Transformation of bad circumstances
into the Way of Enlightenment -- When the world
is filled with evil transform all mishaps
into the path of *bodhi*."

At that precise moment I notice
the absence of noise, the new rhythm
of space and silence, the cafeteria cleared.
I feel serene for a second.
Then a family of six sits down beside me --
they are Russian. I am at first enchanted
with the Babushka who brings in the baby,
round and rosey in bright red woolens,
yellow blue and purple cap and pom pom.

He grins at me, sitting plop on the table,
and I grin back!
Then in come young mama and papa,
uncle and grandpa, pulling out
cheese sandwiches for the family picnic.
I want to tell them: "I'm on my way
to where you've been. I'm going to
the place you've left! Look!
My maps! St. Petersburg! Moskva!"
But I smile and send simple well-wishes
instead while they finish. I feel

a part of their feast, a privileged
neighbor, and edge contentedly against
their enjoyment of each other's company.

I read on, vision blurred
from a sleepless night on the plane
from Portland (and another to go!
forty-four hours awake) --
"Sending and taking should be
practised alternately.
These two should ride the breath . . .
Begin the sequence of sending and
taking with oneself."

I've made the first friends
of my trip without leaving
New York, but it is not
the New York of three hours ago.
Already I have entered
a new world.

GHOSTS

At the airport, arriving
visitors are on their own.
Squeeze onto the bus: there is only the one.
This is a vestige of the Leningrad
of years, not months, ago.

The handsome soldiers in fur hats,
high boots and long brown and red coats,
the officials -- they stomp in the cold
or sit, heads bowed, in shadows
against the walls.

Once in these corners
people came and went
in silent exhaustion,
separated from their loved ones
forever, sometimes brought back
to become mere property of the state themselves.

On the straight wooden benches
empty now I see them clearly,
sitting in colorless resignation,
waiting, listening for their name
to be called for the final time,
where terror and destiny
made an evil pact
of submission and despair.

ST. PETERSBURG -- AGAIN

Two cities -- silver St. Petersburg.
Through lace curtains, ice breaks
on the Neva, night traffic drifts
through the new coat of snow.
Across the river, the cemetery,
Nevsky Prospect, the monastery
of Saint Trinity. Vespers.
Flowers sleep
in frozen ground
around the poets' graves.

At dawn one sees
brightly colored western clothes
worn by young people rushing
to work. The old queue up
for boots and bread.
The streets reverberate
with rose-pink palaces,
gods and goddesses who seem
to hold up the green marble
of aristocratic facades.
Yellow and white Italian
architecture echoes the past.
People hurry past, forgetting pride,
rendered small by smoke stacks
pillaring the Leningrad sky.

Five million people,
more than workers,
individuals with lives --
all on their way to the factory,
the outdated nuclear plant
where radiation overshadows
the Baltic Sea, and everywhere
battered buildings beg:
learn to care for yourselves.

11

BREAKFAST IN ST. PETERSBURG

Two small white feet peek
from under a white satin
nightgown. The woman draped
in a black and gold shawl
sits curled by the window.
She turns toward the world
in the half-dark of night's end.
The dawn fog on the Neva River,
night lights suddenly blink off
at seven, the bridge fills
with workers using only their
parking lights. Unable to see
they move hesitantly
among buses and trollies,
finding their way
by braille or memory.
The white sky and white ground merge.
Somewhere invisible between,
the river groans, breaks open
and moves.

       Ice breaks apart, releases
       the river in pieces
       of lifeflow, sudden, sporadic,
       uncertain -- then swelling itself
       lets go into the rare, ecstatic
       waves of first true melt.

The woman is foreign, yet familiar,
first generation émigrée, she returns
yet has never been here.
Her blood remembers her mother's stories,
and shudders and swells through her body
for reasons she only can feel.

In morning half-light she hungers,
eats chocolate from home, drinks
cool tapwater tea.
A sealed bottle of Portuguese wine
rests on the table.
Soon she dresses,
descends to the ground floor,
joins others for breakfast.

They are in a banquet room,
their plush red chairs under
elaborate chandeliers, murals
of Old Russia surround them --
skaters, cupolas, boats on the river,
gleaming deep red, cerulean, gold.
Beside them a white grand piano
is closed.

The woman announces
to her travel companions,
"This morning I heard church bells
and the birds singing."
Her friends regard her as if
they are seeing a ghost.
She realizes: *no birds have returned.*
It is too soon.
The bells I heard belong
to a hundred years ago.
I am listening to my mother's dream.

> Through the open window
> snow strikes her face.
> She shakes herself.
> Outside a crow laughs.

> *If the grey and black*
> *crow plays already in the snow,*
> *can the yellow songbird*
> *be far behind?*

13

The twelfth-century bell tower in Cathedral Square, the Kremlin. In the spring of 1992, for the first time since 1917, it rang out at midnight, Easter Eve, the first peal of the Resurrection, signaling the other 1600 bells of Moscow to join in the jubilant sounds.

AT THE BEGINNING

"Now we have to invent ourselves."

This is no place for the sensitive --
But we're all sensitive here!
Inhaling poisons
our greed and fear have created,
we try to remember how to be bold.
We choke on the air,
the rusty waters gag us
with what we imagine.
Everything post-war is new and
looks twice as old as what is left
of the last century.

Take heart. Remember that you loved
beauty once. Let the ugliness
and dirt of this century wash away
with the spring rains.
Brown earth will green over
and live again.
You will live again!

EARLY SPRING, 1992 -- CHANGE

Ludmilla the tour guide
and Misha the bus driver
are gentle and bubbling
with anger and tentative hope.
Sensitive and proud, they confess,
"At least when we had no freedom
we ate -- Now we are free but hungry.
So how are we free? To choose
between starving alone or together?
Everything's changed again!"
Yes, but -- with this
freedom you can create something --
yourselves.

PRAYER OVER BENDED BACKS

Spring, we ask
one gift of you
this year --
let the sunflowers
stay in their fields
and with them
let us lift
our faces to the sun.

AWAKE

My friends sleeps.
Soon she will forget
how to sleep.
I slept three hours
in three days.
I walk around the hotel room
with a light at my chest,
a secret coal miner of the heart,
searching the corners
to find fuel from the darkness
of deep night.
Stale cigarette smoke permeates
everything -- blankets, curtains, walls.
Gagging and choking, my eyes swollen
and weeping, I open the window
to the river, let in
the sweet air of fresh snowfall.
Make orange tea from rusty tapwater.
It is warm! Make it good as well!
Improvise! Adjust! Invent!
Imagine! Create! Just as if
you lived here.

AT THE BALLET

In Petersburg
at the Little Ballet
a large white angel flies
in each corner of the stage,
blessing the wings
of the theatre and all
who leap and exult there,
all who fall weary
into the wild ovations
of entranced audiences
like me, unable to move
or acknowledge it's over,
refusing to go home,
at dawn still sitting there,
throwing roses at the dancers' feet.

TRANSCENDENCE AND NECESSITY

In my winter white fur hat
I absorb a little of the reality
of cultural necessity:
here animals share more than flesh
for survival.

Everyone here reads the bible
and knows the stories better
than dreams, but only ten percent
believe in God.
What resounds for them is
exodus and resurrection.

The day we leave for home
trouble starts in the city.
The young turn old in a day,
they shrink into the vastness
of an inner tundra, try to resist
gravity. Aching bones muster
strength and spirit from somewhere
to take a stand, find a voice,
actively shape a good day.

MOTHER RUSSIA

At the Russian Museum we see images
of madness and mercy -- Prince Paul
the hate-child, malignant narcissist,
and barefooted Tolstoy the farmer
tending the land in old age.
Not different now -- to arrive
at the old Leningrad airport one sees
the frozen countenances of old hostility
and fear deeply masking a young woman's face.
She could be beautiful.
Her first smile will make her so.
Still, she regards the stranger
with justified suspicion.
She sits listless in a Customs room
where hard benches stick
on dirty bloodstained floors
which do nothing now but hold up
the tired walls.

When leaving, the visitor is taken
to a new section not seen before,
the St. Petersburg version of a modern
airport: grey marble obscures
the still-filthy floors.
But one sees a few smiles,
an ice cream and espresso bar,
people traveling with their pets --
a small white cat in particular --
and treasures of Russia beautify
the gift shop: cobalt blue goblets
with white serpentine stems,
laquered eggs, amber perfumes and
reproductions of icons in porcelain
and gold.

On the streets we have seen
a steady assault of capitalist hustlers
pushing matrushka dolls and laquered boxes,
the occasional hand-painted balalaika or mandolin.
Soon the Dutch will take over the bubblegum concession,
and Texans will set up the oil trade.
Meanwhile, at home, Olga is thrilled
to have obtained, after only three hours in line,
a pound of sugar -- the first since last year.
Nevermind its price is 90 rubles, not kopeks as before --
Her mother Tatiana bakes a precious currant cake
to celebrate our visit. Valodya the father shows
us wedding pictures and takes pride in his babies.
Vasya, now a young man of seventeen, plays the saxaphone,
and Irina is in pre-med. They still all live
in two rooms and sleep on fold-down chairs at night.
They try not to inhale the bad air that rises
from the Black River near their home, and stay
indoors for four days following a nuclear accident.

Mother Russia has been raped
by angry sons for generations.
Let her heal and slowly find her way
under gentler hands.

At the Russian Museum stand two seascapes
of equal size side by side:
"The Ninth Wave" and "The Last Wave."
One is of hope, the other, despair.
One of death, the other, resurrection.
The same power is in each,
the same light.
But in one, the boat goes under;
in the other, it rises
from transcendent light
and is carried through to an unseen shore.

RUSSIAN NIGHTS

Stars of the city's
night reflected
in water, lights
crossing the bridge.

I see dawn
on the Neva,
the ice breaking
and more light
coming through
all the time.

Dawn on the Neva River as seen from my window in the Hotel Moskva

EXILES

Baryshnikov
Nureyev
Kandinsky
Chagall

Your memory
is tucked away
in the minds
of your people,
those you had to leave behind.

One day
they will
be able
to hold you
openly
to their hearts
again and
celebrate

your free spirits
with their own.

DIALECTIC

Olga, Tanya, and Vladimir
entertain us expansively
in their two-room flat.
The children, Vasya and Irina
are out taking music lessons
and studying.

We eat potatoes from the country
and cucumbers from town.
Red tulips we have carried
through the deep Underground
open in full glory, yellow
stamen against the gold wallpaper.
Iced cake and samovar tea.
Apples and currants in tall glasses
with fresh sugar just purchased
dearly.

On the way back in the taxi,
Olga whispers when we pass a
medium-sized grey building, "KGB."
I look up as we turn the corner,
see a green plant growing
in a fifth floor window,
white curtains.

The old functions change.
What oppressed now seeks
to protect.

Sometime soon, let freedom
and security breathe as one.

Tea time in the home of Olga Vessart, Black River, St. Petersburg

THE SOURCE

This is a country
whose religion is poetry,
a people in love
with their arts.

Pushkin is saint,
sage, prophet, and seer.
At Black River he died,
shot in a duel for
a woman's honor.

In the Metro station
there a solemn marble
statue honors him.

At the ballet
every evening
they come
for communion.

Children knowing
the score by heart
hum along in bliss
to Tchaikovsky
and grown men weep
openly.

Outside riding home
together they are more stoic
than people riding home
in other cities -- as grey
as Pushkin's statue.
At home with their icons
and children, they gather

angels to their humble tables,
made generous with bread and wine.
They sing their prayers.
They fill themselves with music
and are renewed again.

NOONDAY REQUIEM

Today I buried my mother
in St. Petersburg.

Spring snows have come and gone.
Ice has broken on the Neva.
The marshy earth becomes
black mud and sand
beneath our feet.
All changes, impossibly,
from dark brown to bright green.

On Holy Fools' Feast
I find your grave, Mama,
waiting for you.

Twenty years after
your transfiguration.
I carry your image,
photo of you at fourteen
from Russia, 1923, back again
into Russia, 1992.

Between times
this was Petrograd
and Leningrad, and
endless wars were waged
within the common psyche
of those who remained
and those who left.

Meanwhile, you were driven
half mad by loss, left,
married, gave birth,
lived and died as best you could.

I buried you in exile
in Canada near your mother
and the sea.

Today you return through me
to your source, the land
of your birth, our Mother Country.
Fate placed me in a hotel
across the Nevsky Prospect
from the monastic cemetery
of Alexander Nevsky.
To the left, Pushkin's family.
To the right, Dostoyevsky,
Tchaikovsky, Rimsky-Korsakov.
Borodin's tombstone is a gilded
score of his song, "Stranger
in Paradise."

The decision is easy --
all the laughing rich bells
of the Easter Liturgy call me
to entrust you to the white stone
cross (your body in White Rock*) --
enclosed in an ancient circle
surrounded by angels, the evangelists,
Mary and Nicholas, Christ in the center.
I kneel to dig a small place for you
near Rimsky-Korsakov's head.
I give you back.
With hot tears I melt the snow
that blankets your earth.
Receive your daughter,
Mother Russia.
She's come home.

*White Rock, British Columbia

Burying Mama's photograph taken of her at the age of 14 in Odessa

Tchaikovsky's grave, the Lora Cemetery

NIGHT TRAIN TO MOSCOW -- 1992

Not the Soviet train
through East Germany
of twenty-six years ago,
with its mustard tin walls
and ghastly blue vinyl seats,
pouring rain all night
from Hamburg to Berlin.
Out the window only barbed wire
visible in the red neon light
at the stations.
Persistent thoughts of relatives
in Siberia loomed in my mind.
Suffocating.

Now in Russia I take
the modern midnight train
from Petersburg to Moscow.
Though nothing matches,
the effort is here:
an oriental rug in each
compartment, walnut veneer walls,
Italian opera on the radio,
reading lights, and no interruption
of soldiers all night long.

RED SQUARE

In Red Square
not beauty*
but blood,
not joy
but evil
perversity.
The terrible love
of gratuitous killing.
The teeth of death gleam
everywhere.

> The scimitar
> the whip
> the scaffold
> the worship of guns.
> Even the children
> wear suits of armor.

*red meant *beautiful*

"WORKERS OF THE WORLD, FORGIVE ME"

Nobody gets it.
None of my friends, anyway.
They must be closet Marxists.
His statue faces the Bolshoi
Ballet Theatre and someone
has written this graffiti
below it and Americans
don't get it.
Idealistic Americans.
Idealistic Marx.
Yes, he was a prophet,
and therein the harm.
It wasn't his fault
that humankind is not ready
for his message, not grown up
enough to live in the true
mutuality of sharing, caring,
and daring respect.
He didn't dream
of totalitarian abuses,
harsh rulers, sadists
and madmen in charge
of the masses, the death camps,
gulags, colorless cities,
people depressed and despairing,
institutionalized dependency,
socialized infantilism.
He dreamt of the dignity
of work and truly shared
responsibility.
Barefooted farmer Tolstoy
might have been his patron saint.
But he spoke too soon,
the devil as ever in charge

of the timing.
He gave out the blueprint
to children who built the machine
and drove it like greedy infants:
wreckless, solipsistic, afraid.
Not yet co-ordinated
they merely had accidents.
It isn't Marx who failed, but we.
He merely spoke too soon.

ON THE STREETCAR

On the streetcar,
in the streets and shops,
on the walks -- still no release,
no hint of engagement
no opening of person
to person, no smile
or expression.

Only the pleading eyes
of beggars, and their gratitude.
Or Gypsy's sly victory betrayed
in the square at midnight,
invisible as stealing hands.

It takes years
to undo the centuries
of harm.
The soul is a fragile
treasure.
It has been collectively
stolen times too often.

MISHA

The affable
young man
who speaks
for his country
and teaches
strangers its ways
gives us a link:
there are no natives
anywhere.

He, afterall, is
a true Russian:
half Tartar, a quarter
Kurd, a quarter Jewish.
Naturally, he mixes
his religions also.
He is an honest citizen
of the world.

AT THE MOSCOW CIRCUS

The armadillo act
and educated bears
precede the little red hen
pulling her wagon --

then ten thousand flutters
and ten thousand magical eyes
when the ringmaster's green and gold
cape opens and the shimmering peacock appears.

IMAGINE

Russian soldiers playing
"The Star Spangled Banner"
for American tourists
in St. Petersburg --
This ain't the Twilight Zone.
Life may be weird and is,
but folks is folks
and Hooray for it!

Music at the Summer Palace

MILLA

She is proud
of her home --
one hundred square meters
for a family of four.

She longs
for spring and signs
of the ground giving up
its impenetrable cold.

She will travel
by train and bus
and on foot at the last,
burdened with gear,
the one hundred kilometers
north of here to her garden.

Escaping the density
of the city
with others she will
begin her planting.
She will grow
living things
and plan
her summer home.

She will build
her dream
and in ten years
or twenty she will
move fully
into it.

HOTEL MOSKVA

The entire fourth floor
of Hotel Moskva is given over
to prostitutes of all ages.
We spent six days on the fifth floor
and were told this as we left.

To be sure, the elevator
rides were an adventure --
Dutch and Finnish men each
at different times with the same
Russian beauty in leather hot pants
and magenta shirt. Soldiers, also.
Here, a woman in one night
made enough money to feed her family
for six months.
Some of them are grandmothers.
They wear bright Russian red
and drape themselves lavishly
in scarves.
These are the ones who run
down the halls, singing.

HOTEL ASTORIA

When it was Hotel Angleterre
Isadora Duncan's husband
killed himself here.
Sergei Yesyinin was his name,
a fine poet of his generation.

On the other side recently
refurbished in turn-of-the-century
refinement, an elegant white grand piano
presides, proud for escaping three wars.
On its side in gold, the goddess Hestia
is served by her hearth-keepers.

The old statues and treasures
are gone -- disappeared with remodeling.
In the English Bar, two drunks
chain-drinking vodka make a game
flicking their big linen bibs
at each other, trailing escargot.
Here and now one drunk Russian
is worth six sober trombones.
More than the poet's life is outpoured.

GRAND HOTEL EUROPISKAYA

Passion fruit torte
with vanilla bean sauce
and raspberry liqueur,
brown sugar cubes with tea
after Norwegian poached salmon
in true Hollandaise.
Morrel mushroom soup
with sour cream and steak
Tartar with French wine.

On the platform in stained glass
peacock motif, a grand piano sings
with violin.

Nearby, a beautiful young woman
interprets in Russian, matching
gesture for gesture, the big
business deal the wealthy Iraqi
is trying to negotiate.
In a hidden alcove, buoyant
laughter takes over
as six ex-peasant Russian
entrepreneurs celebrate
the first tastes of capitalism.

AT THE SUMMER PALACE

Tsarskoe Selo --
the mother land
of Pushkin's poetry
and Akhmatova's spiritual
home.

Versailles of the north,
the Russian jewel.

My friend Julia and I
dance in the snow here
among linden trees,
down through rows of birch,
their white and black radiance
astounding in winter sunlight.

The band members look warm
in their red and brown uniforms.
A grey and black crow plays
with the dogs.

As we glide down the slopes
Our guide explains the greatness
of the Russian crow:
"Only the most intelligent
animals can be observed
at play."

MOTHER TONGUE

They come back,
those words and phrases,
even the lullabyes
from early childhood,
echoes of the land
of my mother's birth.

The language of Russia
gently erupts in me,
though I must constantly
ask for translation
of the words I speak.

I remember the baby songs
the best, with words
that need no translation.
What mind utters from memory
heart instantly understands.

Stammering now like
a toddler in the mother tongue
I give back as best I can:
"Spasibo. Blago slavi tibi Boje."
Thank you. God bless you.

GOODBYE

A red disc rises
over the Neva.
The water is not well.
The air chokes on itself.
It is time to say
Goodbye.

God, let these living
beings live again.
Remind them how to help
all creation renew itself --
remind us also,
all people, all lands,
together.

BACK TO KENNEDY AIRPORT, NEW YORK

At the terminal
things end:
waiting, patience,
strength, endurance.

A fifteen-year old girl
and her baby, blonde and raven-haired
at the gate -- a royal personage
from Africa in white robes and
ostrich plumes, his noble hat
of burgundy and silver --
a tall distinguished looking
grey-haired man, slender,
smoking slowly and gracefully
a long cigarette, walking
barefoot through the end zone,
utterly vacant eyes.

AT THE END

Alone in New York
at the airport, checking
for departure gates,
I read my home destination
then below it, Paris and Tel Aviv --
all the same gate.

One gate leads to and from
many times and places.
What matters is not how many times
we go through, but with what insight
and decision to change our lives
we learn to return.

Another forty-four hours pass
on the long journey home.
At last, my spring garden
welcomes me like a pink and purple,
green and red brass band, and
the tiny wildflowers sing in tones of blue.
In dawn light the birds lift up
their violin voices.
Inside, the house hugs me to itself
and I join the chorus.
With happiness and gratitude
I feel my belonging here.

At midnight the telephone rings.
Wakened from the deep sleep
of journey's end I hear my friend's words
from a street corner in Tel Aviv:
"Welcome home!" he says.

Afterword

UNCLE YASHA, or MY FAMILY HISTORY

Why is the world so full
of widows and pregnant women?
And the world of books also
full of them?
Children orphaned
by husbands and wives --
girl widows and boy widows
everywhere. And always
more coming:
How many wombs are
filled with widows?
How many widows' wombs?

Despite what the dust jacket says
the book is about (: all kinds
of love, including love as a
disease), I have discovered
on page 288 what *Love in the Time
of Cholera* is about -- it is
the history of an obsession
with the past, a refusal
of the old century to die
and its persistence in burying
itself alive in the minds
of the denizens of the author's
homeland. His birth country bears
the past through an insistence
on memory as current fact.

My Uncle Yasha came to dinner
this evening. He is eighty years
old to my forty. We drank
the rhubarb wine he brought and
ate outside and watched

the sun go down on the mountain.
He counted my roses and told me
stories about gathering 10,000
eggs a day in rural Russia
nearly a century ago.
Then he asked, "Will you marry
again or live alone always?"

I said, looking away, "I am
loved. I must wait. I do
not want to be alone always . . . .
And what about you?"

"I'm too old and too poor
for an American wife. Besides,
I have too many grandchildren!"

Stars began to blink above us
in green and gold. I asked,
"Where did my mother stay
when she went to school in Moscow?"
"Moscow? She was never in Moscow.
Was she? Maybe. I don't remember.
Why ask now? Why didn't you
ask her?"

"I was too young."
"How old were you when she died?"
"Twenty-four."
"That was too young?"

"The young always look forward.
Only the aging look back
and hunger for family history,
and then it's too late.
It died with my mother's memory.

I come from nowhere
I know and go the same."

"Even the old
can look forward," he said.

GENERATION

I

An old man in black
shrunken into yourself,
you sit alone
in the front pew
at your brother's funeral,
holding the hymnal,
your bowed head
still.

> "It is well
>   it is well
> In my soul
>   in my soul
> It is well in my soul
>   it is well."

Words wing around
your silent ears,
lips, hands.
You hold time
to your breast,
place pieces of time
in your pockets.

At the end
you blow your nose,
stand, hobble after all
the others, wave your cane
in the air to greet me,
your long-dead cousin's daughter.

You enter my open arms
with words, determined,

intentional: "I am the last
of the old ones"
You say it without punctuation,
like an open-ended proclamation.
I hold you tight to my breast,
unwilling to inherit the mantle
of elder.

Your death will mean
my old age.
I am not ready.

On the way
to the cemetery we pass
the Pioneer Graveyard,
full of Chinese workers'
bones from the last century.
Then White Birch Cemetery
and the names of Europe
and Russia: The Snow Family.

Under the pavillion
I wait alone, remembering
four years ago when we all
stood here and your brother's
three sons held him back
from throwing his body
into their mother's grave,
his loud cries for her
to take him.
At last he can follow.
I glance down and see
near my feet five sand dollars,
starshells that a child would love --
a green and silver pinwheel blowing
fresh from the beach, planted in grass

over two fawns engraved in stone --
the name --

> Christopher Robert Dickey
> Ours to love forever.
> November 19, 1980-
> April 9, 1986

In the sweet September rain
a silver toy spins
to entertain the spirits.

The others come, you no longer alone,
leaning on your daughter's arm,
your long black coat touching
your farmer's Sunday shoes,
your face more grey than white
above your charcoal collar.
My foot slips.
I look down and see on wet marble
the name of your wife, my mother's friend,
and beside it, under my toe,
the smooth and empty place
where your name will be.

II

At the reception
back at church, we see your history
in pictures, your families linked
through time and trial.
You and your brother were refugees
forty years ago, now retired Oregon berry farmers.
Your children's children prosper
and their children play
at your feet.

Your daughter's mother-in-law
explains to me again
how her son is also my second cousin --
your daughter on my grandfather's side,
her husband on my grandmother's:

Your father and Mama's father were brothers.
His grandmother and my grandmother were sisters.
I am second cousin to both wife and husband.
Anna, the mother, reminds me that I wore
yellow (the only time in my life)
at her son's wedding, a bridesmaid.
I was eleven years old.
Their grandchildren run by us and giggle.

Anna and I eat cherry cake, drink coffee
and fresh berry juice from the farm.
She tells me the stories of old Russia
at each family gathering.
She is the keeper of memories.
Today she says,

      "When I was a girl and young wife
      in Russia, I baked the best bread --
      oh! I shouldn't brag!"

      "Go ahead," I say.

      "Well -- the other woman, much older,
      could never get it right. I was ashamed
      when her husband praised my perfect bread
      to scold her. But it really was perfect!
      So round and high . . .
      We made our own yeast then, from corn mash
      and bamboo flowers, stored with hops
      under a willow tree. The *chleb* came out

golden from my outdoor summer oven.
The children begged for my shiny braided *kalach* . . ."

A sad radiance comes over her.
Without breaking communion
we gather ourselves
slowly into the present.
"May I take you home?" I ask.
"Thank you, Alla." She kisses me.
I hold time tight in my arms,
accepting my legacy.

THE DANCE --
All Saints' Night

When I was three, Mama took me for the first
of a hundred times to the Nicholas Vasiliev School of Ballet
in the Hollywood District of Portland.
My soul remembers the possibility of dance once felt in my bones.
Today the promise was realized fully, but beyond my own body.
Today the Bolshoi has come to Portland.

I did not see them, these great ones, these eleven
athletes of God, in Moscow, but as distinguished guests
in my own hometown. They honor my birthplace, all Grace
outpouring, they begin with a tribute to the great Ulanova,
paying homage to all spiritual ancestors and teachers of Grace.
Body-rich angels before me in human form gather the Powers,
their energies leaping into matter in transcendent communion.

Danseur noble and *prima ballerina assoluta* are here --
one-hundred-seven-years of living combined in gracious presence.
She is fifty-four, he is fifty-three:
> Ekaterina Maximova and Vladimir Vasiliev

She wears a dress of stars.
He is Apollo, golden with age
in a garment of night.
Together they entwine and fly
through heaven, carrying us
on their wings.

All nerve and blood, they move, are perfectly
still, together. They are mother/father
as one. They are forever in love.

It is they who bring us
to our feet in tears,

not the young ones
with all their beauty
and virtuosity.
It is these wise and weathered
faces where we see the story
their bodies tell, going to the center
of Earth and past the boundaries of cosmos.
The scrolls of experience unfold:
in mid-air pause, a moment, eternity --
she the Shekinah, he her consort,
an old Jewish couple reliving their lifetime together:
the losses, the joys, all reconciled in their delicate dance.
The feathery fingers barely touch and we know all, all,
more than could ever be told, all remembered in these forms,
moving as one in human skin, a divine inkling,
color leaving, returning, as they show us
the mystery contained in their years.
A solid strength and deep fragility of being.

You cannot describe it, this fusion of passion and power.
It is not to be understood. The old ones who are whole
show it forth -- a shining.

All opposites married, holy at last,
they dance a spontaneous union of elements --
Earth, Fire, Water, Wind, and Beyond.
They offer it to us generously, endlessly,
the life that is God in all life,
beginning, beginning.

Also by Alla Renée Bozarth

BOOKS

Womanpriest: A Personal Odyssey
The Word's Body: An Incarnational Aesthetic of Interpretation
Life is Goodbye/Life is Hello: Grieving Well through All Kinds of Loss
A Journey through Grief
Love's Prism: Reflections from the Heart of a Woman
At the Foot of the Mountain: Discovering Images for Emotional Healing

Poetry

Gynergy
In the Name of the Bee & the Bear & the Butterfly
Sparrow Songs (a father-daughter collaboration with René Bozarth)
Stars in Your Bones: Emerging Signposts on Our Spiritual Journeys (with visual artist Julia Barkley and cultural historian Terri Hawthorne)

AUDIOTAPES

A Journey through Grief
Dance for Me When I Die: Death as a Rite of Passage
Water Women
Reading Out Loud to God
All Shall Be Well, All Shall Be One